The Edible Pyramid

GOOD EATING EVERY DAY

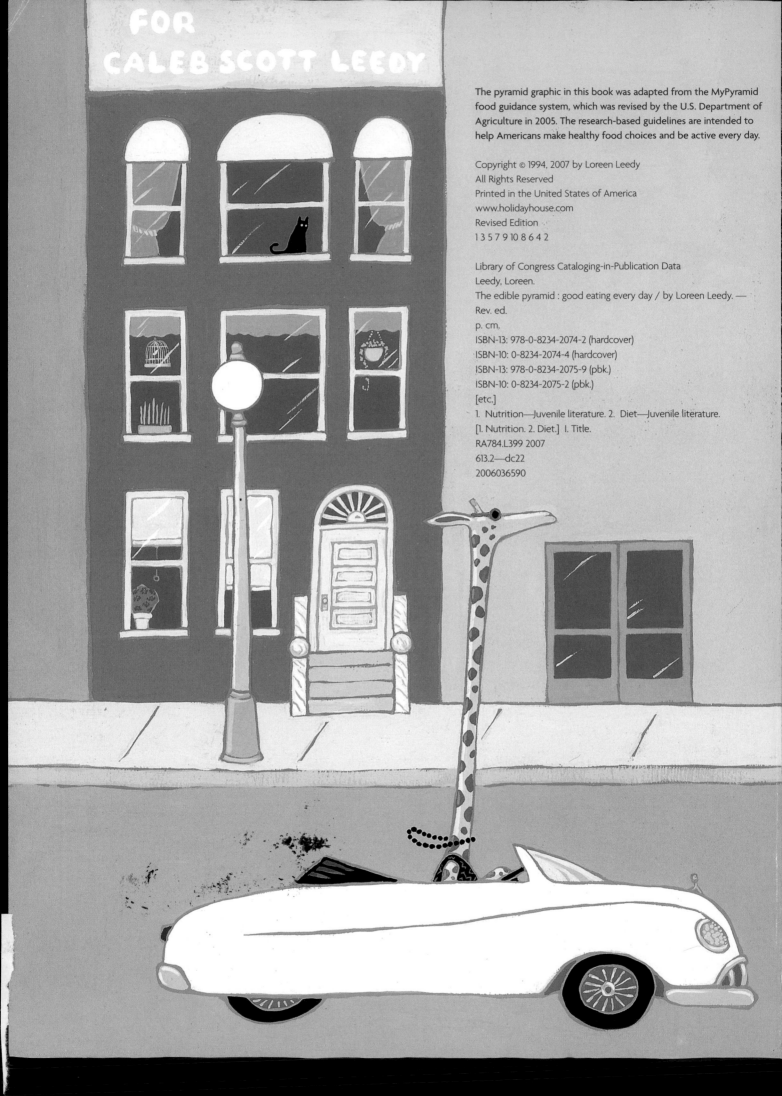

FOR
CALEB SCOTT LEEDY

The pyramid graphic in this book was adapted from the MyPyramid food guidance system, which was revised by the U.S. Department of Agriculture in 2005. The research-based guidelines are intended to help Americans make healthy food choices and be active every day.

Library of Congress Cataloging-in-Publication Data
Leedy, Loreen.
The edible pyramid : good eating every day / by Loreen Leedy. — Rev. ed.
p. cm.
ISBN-13: 978-0-8234-2074-2 (hardcover)
ISBN-10: 0-8234-2074-4 (hardcover)
ISBN-13: 978-0-8234-2075-9 (pbk.)
ISBN-10: 0-8234-2075-2 (pbk.)
[etc.]
1. Nutrition—Juvenile literature. 2. Diet—Juvenile literature.
[1. Nutrition. 2. Diet.] I. Title.
RA784.L399 2007
613.2—dc22
2006036590

The Edible Pyramid

GOOD EATING — EVERY DAY

written & illustrated by

Loreen Leedy

Holiday House · New York

On the day of the grand opening of The Edible Pyramid restaurant, customers lined up to get inside.

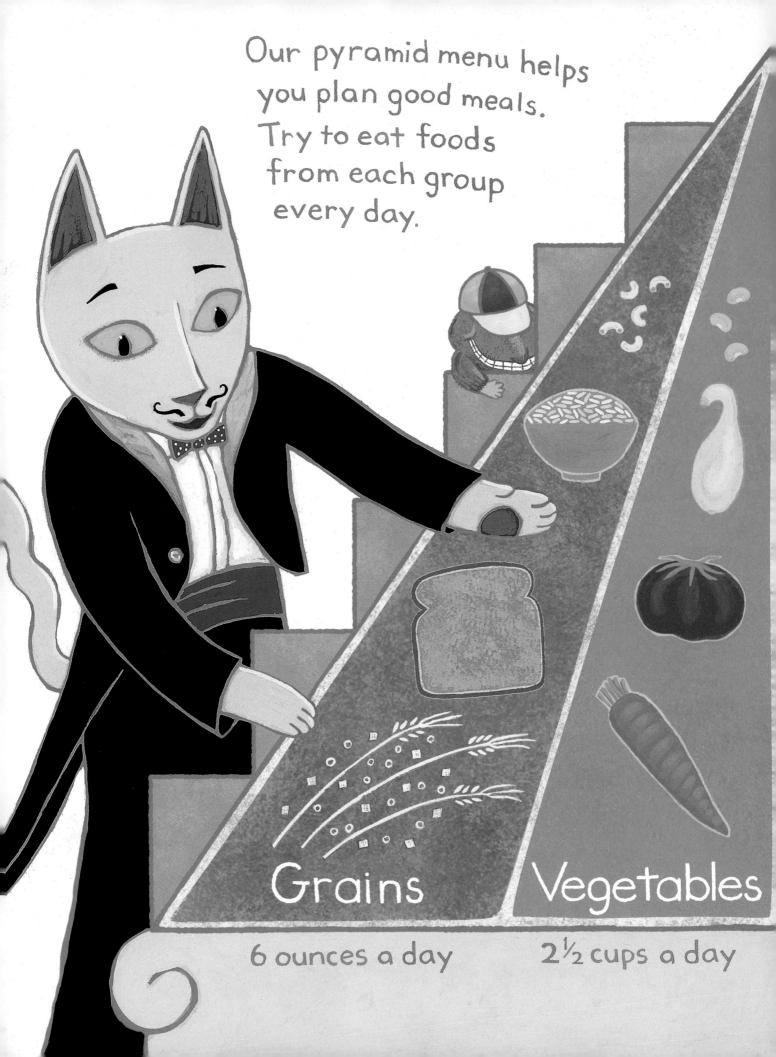

Our pyramid menu helps
you plan good meals.
Try to eat foods
from each group
every day.

Grains

Vegetables

6 ounces a day

2½ cups a day

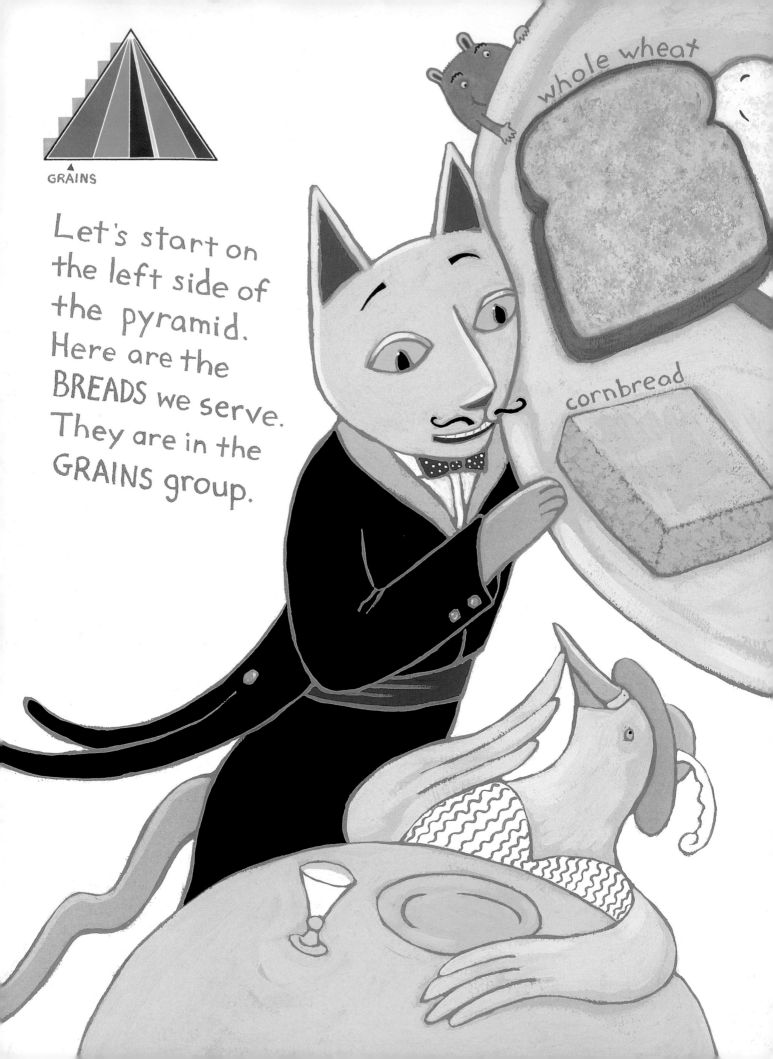

GRAINS

Let's start on the left side of the pyramid. Here are the BREADS we serve. They are in the GRAINS group.

whole wheat

cornbread

VEGETABLES

Now we move over a row in the pyramid. VEGETABLES come in delicious colors.

tomato

eggplant

peas

carrot

broccoli

corn on the cob

potato

onion

peach

cherry

banana

cantaloupe

apple

lemon

strawberry

Swiss cheese

cream cheese

Cheddar cheese

mozzarella cheese

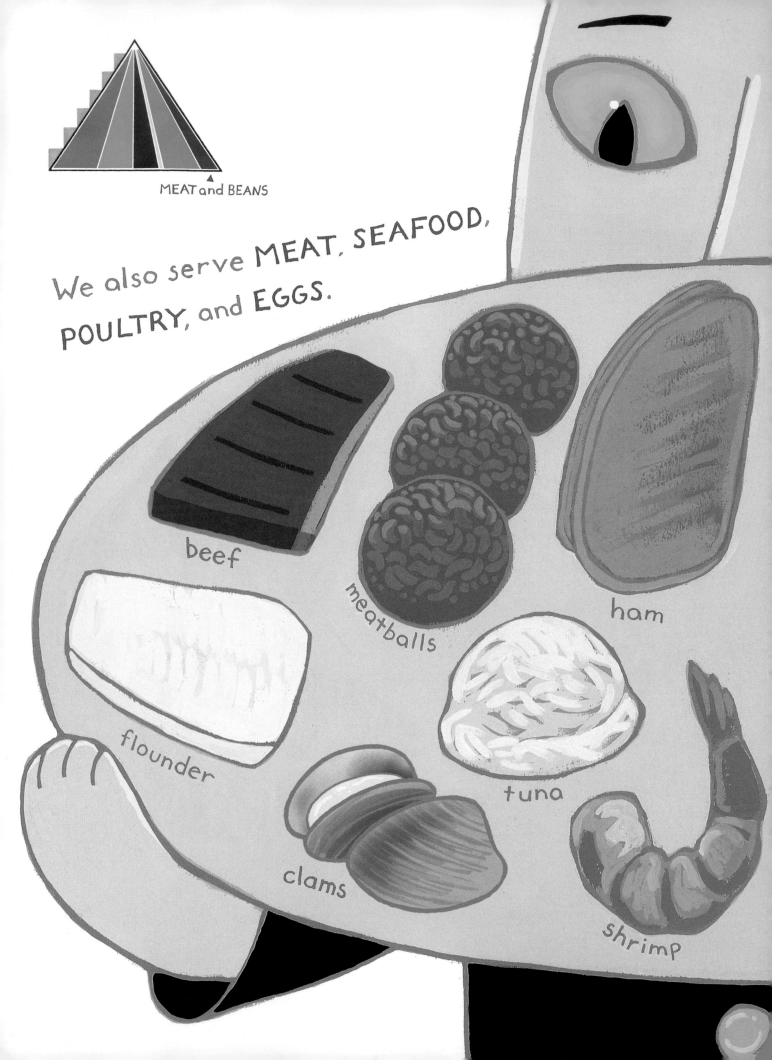

MEAT and BEANS

We also serve MEAT, SEAFOOD, POULTRY, and EGGS.

beef

meatballs

ham

flounder

tuna

clams

shrimp

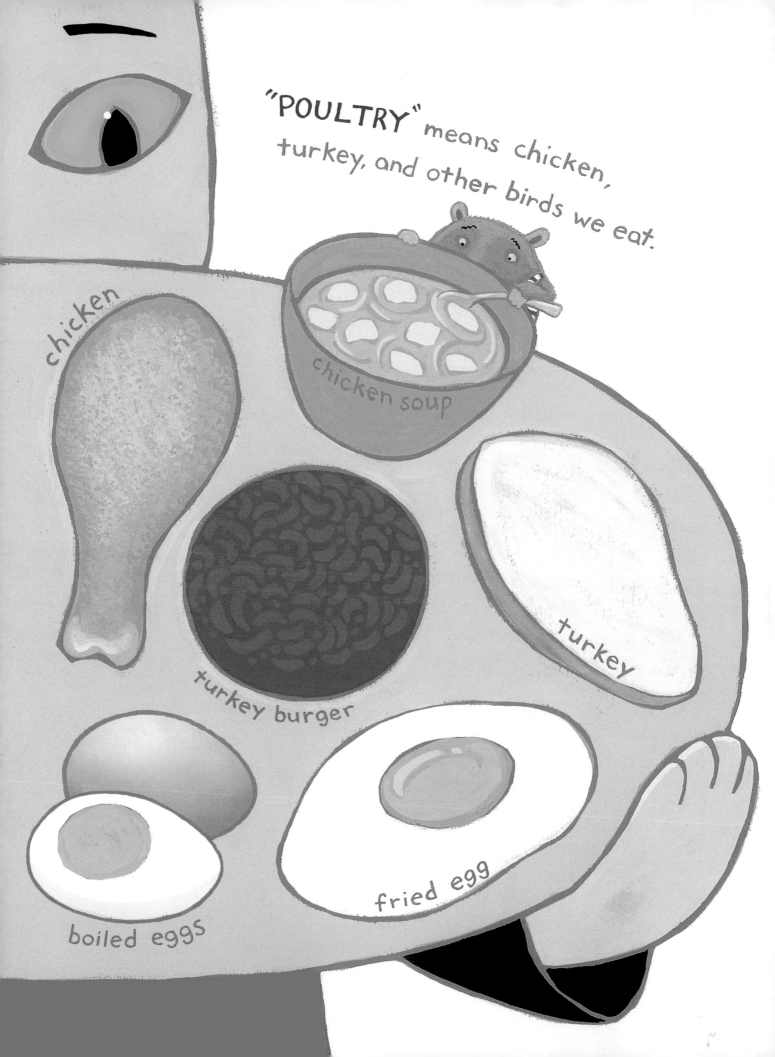

"POULTRY" means chicken, turkey, and other birds we eat.

chicken

chicken soup

turkey

turkey burger

boiled eggs

fried egg

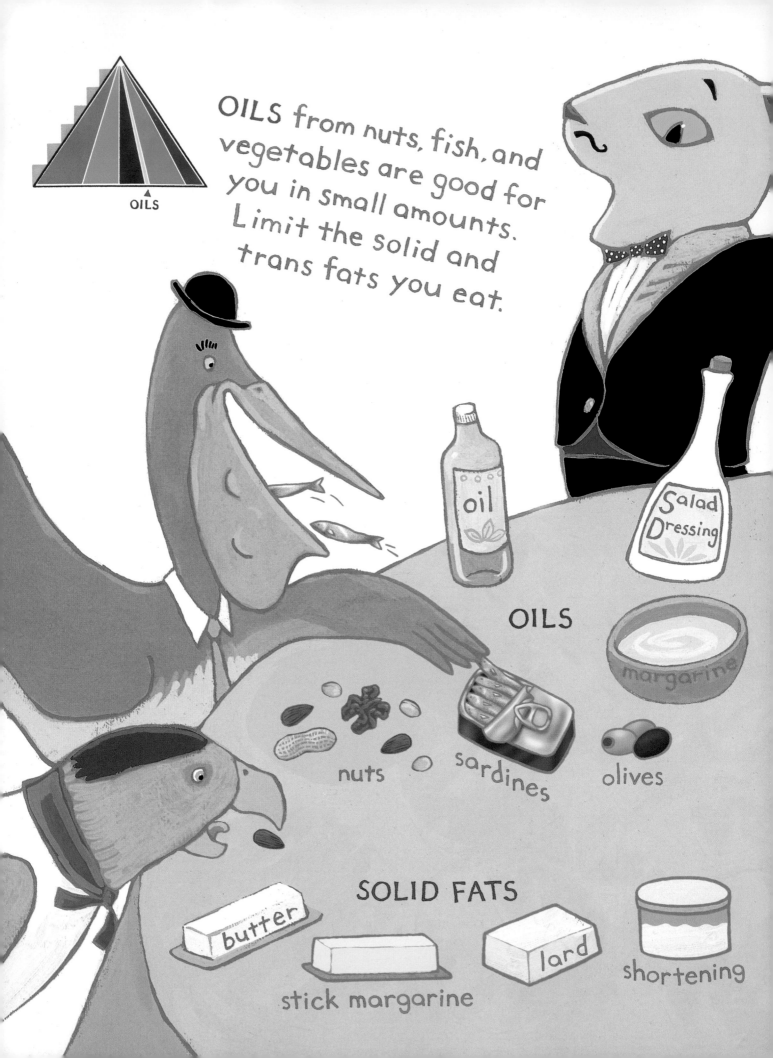

If you eat many sweets and fats, you may gain too much weight.

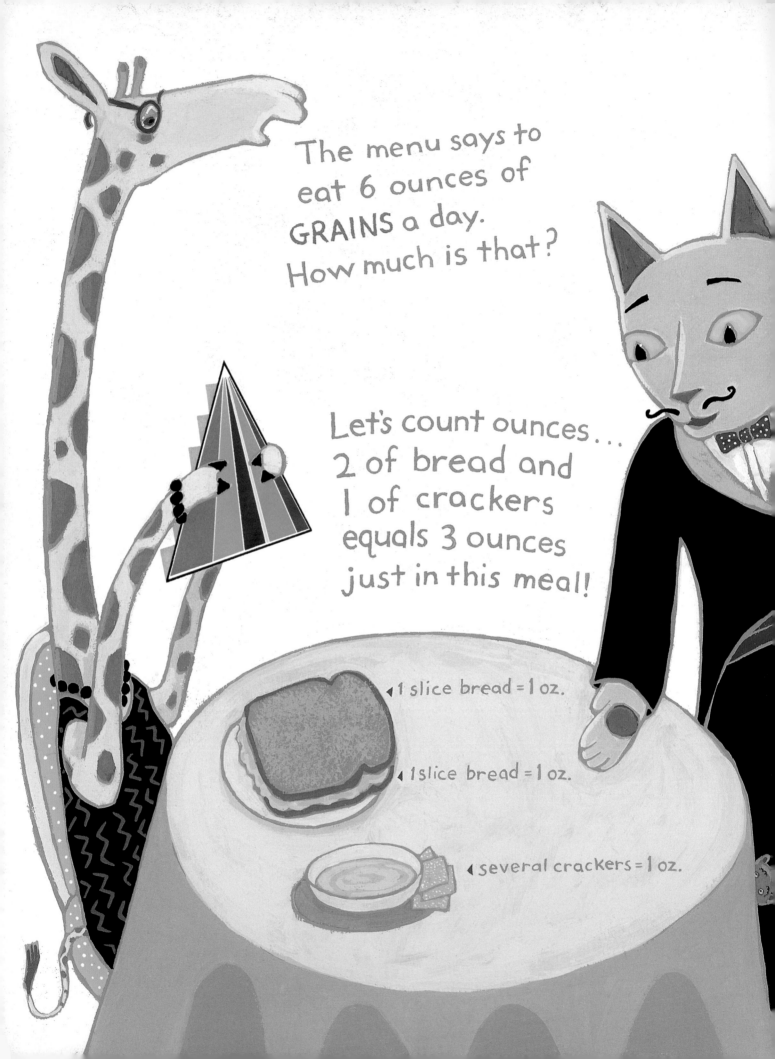

The menu says to eat 6 ounces of GRAINS a day. How much is that?

Let's count ounces... 2 of bread and 1 of crackers equals 3 ounces just in this meal!

◄ 1 slice bread = 1 oz.

◄ 1 slice bread = 1 oz.

◄ several crackers = 1 oz.

Sometimes foods are mixed together, such as in pizza. Just estimate how much of each food group is in your serving.

Kids should exercise for at least one hour every day. But let's finish eating first!